W9-CPE-234

Major US Historical Wars

WORLD WAR II

Jim Corrigan

Mason Crest
Philadelphia

Mason Crest
450 Parkway Drive, Suite D
Broomall, PA 19008
www.masoncrest.com

Printed and bound in the United States of America.
CPSIA Compliance Information: Batch #MUW2015.
For further information, contact Mason Crest at 1-866-MCP-Book.

3 5 7 9 8 6 4 2
Library of Congress Cataloging-in-Publication Data

ISBN:978-1-4222-3363-4 (hc)
ISBN: 978-1-4222-8603-6 (ebook)

Major US Historical Wars series ISBN: 978-1-4222-3352-8

Picture Credits: Library of Congress: 15, 17, 33, 49; National Archives: 9, 11, 13, 18, 20, 22, 24, 31, 38, 40, 48, 50, 53, 55; National Guard Heritage Collection: 29, 43; Everett Historical / Shutterstock: 46; Marco Rubino / Shutterstock.com: 1; U.S. Military Acad- emy: 25; U.S. Naval History and Heritage Command: 7, 27, 35, 56.

About the Author: Jim Corrigan has authored dozens of books for young readers, as well as a regimental history for Civil War enthusiasts. His specialties include history, technology, and medicine. He holds an M.A. in Writing from Johns Hopkins University, and resides in Pennsylvania with his wife, Connie..

TABLE OF CONTENTS

KEY ICONS TO LOOK FOR:

Text-dependent questions: These questions send the reader back to the text for more careful attention to the evidence presented there.

Words to understand: These words with their easy-to-understand definitions will increase the reader's understanding of the text, while building vocabulary skills.

Series glossary of key terms: This back-of-the book glossary contains terminology used throughout this series. Words found here increase the reader's ability to read and comprehend higher-level books and articles in this field.

Research projects: Readers are pointed toward areas of further inquiry connected to each chapter. Suggestions are provided for projects that encourage deeper research and analysis.

Sidebars: This boxed material within the main text allows readers to build knowledge, gain insights, explore possibilities, and broaden their perspectives by weaving together additional information to provide realistic and holistic perspectives.

Other Titles in This Series

Introduction

by Series Consultant Jason Musteen

Lt. Col. Jason R. Musteen is a U.S. Army Cavalry officer and combat veteran who has held various command and staff jobs in Infantry and Cavalry units. He holds a PhD in Napoleonic History from Florida State University and currently serves as Chief of the Division of Military History at the U.S. Military Academy at West Point. He has appeared frequently on the History Channel.

Why should middle and high school students read about and study American wars? Does doing so promote militarism or instill misguided patriotism? The United States of America was born at war, and the nation has spent the majority of its existence at war. Our wars have demonstrated both the best and worst of who we are. They have freed millions from oppression and slavery, but they have also been a vehicle for fear, racism, and imperialism. Warfare has shaped the geography of our nation, informed our laws, and it even inspired our national anthem. It has united us and it has divided us.

Valley Forge, the *USS Constitution*, Gettysburg, Wounded Knee, Belleau Wood, Normandy, Midway, Inchon, the A Shau Valley, and Fallujah are all a part of who we are as a nation. Therefore, the study of America at war does not necessarily make students or educators militaristic; rather, it makes them thorough and responsible. To ignore warfare, which has been such a significant part of our history, would not only leave our education incomplete, it would also be negligent.

For those who wish to avoid warfare, or to at least limit its horrors, understanding conflict is a worthwhile, and even necessary, pursuit. The American author John Steinbeck once said, "all war is a symptom of man's failure as a thinking animal." If Steinbeck is right, then we must think.

And we must think about war. We must study war with all its attendant horrors and miseries. We must study the heroes and the villains. We must study the root causes of our wars, how we chose to fight them, and what has been achieved or lost through them. The study of America at war is an essential component of being an educated American.

Still, there is something compelling in our military history that makes the study not only necessary, but enjoyable, as well. The desperation that drove Washington's soldiers across the Delaware River at the end of 1776 intensifies an exciting story of American success against all odds. The sailors and Marines who planted the American flag on the rocky peak of Mount Suribachi on Iwo Jima still speak to us of courage and sacrifice. The commitment that led American airmen to the relief of West Berlin in the Cold War inspires us to the service of others. The stories of these men and women are exciting, and they matter. We should study them. Moreover, for all the suffering it brings, war has at times served noble purposes for the United States. Americans can find common pride in the chronicle of the Continental Army's few victories and many defeats in the struggle for independence. We can accept that despite inflicting deep national wounds and lingering division, our Civil War yielded admirable results in the abolition of slavery and eventual national unity. We can celebrate American resolve and character as the nation rallied behind a common cause to free the world from tyranny in World War II. We can do all that without necessarily promoting war.

In this series of books, Mason Crest Publishers offers students a foundation for the study of American wars. Building on the expertise of a team of accomplished authors, the series explores the causes, conduct, and consequences of America's wars. It also presents educators with the means to take their students to a deeper understanding of the material through additional research and project ideas. I commend it to all students and to those who educate them to become responsible, informed Americans.

Chapter 1:

A WORLD ABLAZE

In autumn 1941, America was the last major nation at peace. War had spread all across the globe like wildfire. Armies fought fierce battles in Europe, Asia, and Africa. The world, it seemed, was ablaze.

Most Americans didn't want to get involved. They remembered the horror of the First World War. In that conflict, U.S. soldiers died on distant battlefields for no clear reason. Americans didn't want to repeat

(Above) American sailors in a small boat rescue a survivor from the water near the sunken battleship USS West Virginia. *The surprise Japanese attack on the U.S. Navy base at Pearl Harbor was intended to cripple the American fleet in the Pacific. In response, the United States declared war on Japan and its allies, entering the Second World War.*

WORDS TO UNDERSTAND IN THIS CHAPTER

aggressive—forceful and warlike.

torpedo—a cigar-shaped missile that propels itself through water.

U-boat—short for the German word *Unterseeboot*, or under-sea boat.

that nightmare. Vast oceans separated them from the current fighting. They felt their country would be safe.

On December 7, 1941, World War II came to America. It happened during a quiet Sunday morning in Hawaii. U.S. Navy ships stood anchored in the shimmering water of Pearl Harbor. The sailors aboard were enjoying a late breakfast.

A heavy drone broke the calm. It sounded like the buzzing of bees. As the hum grew louder, dozens of airplanes appeared in the distance. The sailors were unconcerned. They assumed the planes were American, but they were wrong. Nearly 200 Japanese fighter-bombers and torpedo planes were moving in fast, ready to strike.

Surprise Attack

Suddenly the Japanese airplanes swarmed over Pearl Harbor. They rained down bombs and bullets on the ships. Sailors scrambled to their anti-aircraft guns, but it was too late.

The USS *Arizona* took a fatal hit. A bomb struck its ammunition supplies. The mighty battleship exploded, killing all aboard. Five torpedoes slammed into the USS *Oklahoma*, which rolled over and sank. More than a dozen other ships went to the bottom of the harbor or took heavy damage.

At nearby airfields, U.S. warplanes were blown to pieces before they could take off. A second wave of Japanese planes arrived. They added to the destruction. Fires raged everywhere, and thick plumes of black smoke billowed into the sky.

In less than two hours, Japan had dealt the U.S. Pacific Fleet a crippling blow. Powerful warships became twisted wrecks. More than 2,400 Americans were dead.

America Reacts

News of Pearl Harbor shocked the nation. People huddled around radios and snatched up newspapers. The attack on December 7 changed everything. President Franklin D. Roosevelt called it "a date which will live in infamy." He asked Congress to declare war on Japan. Two nations on Japan's side—Germany and Italy—declared war on the United States. America was fully drawn into World War II.

Pearl Harbor turned out to be just the beginning. Japanese troops were splashing ashore on American islands across the Pacific. They overwhelmed U.S. Marines and soldiers at Wake Island, Guam, and the Philippines. They even landed on Alaska's Aleutian Islands. People feared California, Oregon, or Washington might be next.

Meanwhile, on America's East Coast, a new threat emerged. German submarines—known as U-boats—began sinking ships. The U-boats torpedoed oil tankers and cargo ships sailing coastal routes. People on shore would see orange fireballs on the horizon. The next day, dead sailors would wash up on the beach.

Clearly, America was unprepared for this war. Its enemies—Germany, Japan, and Italy—called themselves

In early 1942, the Japanese military seemed unstoppable. These Japanese troops are celebrating the capture of the Bataan Peninsula on the Philippine Islands.

the Axis powers. They were aggressive and well prepared. On the plus side, America was not alone in this fight. Many nations had already banded together to stop the Axis. Unfortunately, they were not doing very well.

Joining the Allies

The war had begun in Europe during September 1939, two years before Pearl Harbor. At that time France, Poland, and Great Britain were working together. More nations joined them as Axis aggression continued. Soon this group of nations came to be called the Allies.

Many Americans did not want to get involved in the European war. But President Roosevelt wanted to help the Allies. He sent them American weapons and supplies. After Pearl Harbor, the United States formally joined the Allies.

As the calendar turned to 1942, the Allies faced a daunting task. Germany and Italy had captured most of continental Europe, as well as North Africa. Meanwhile, Japan's military pushed deeper into Asia and the Pacific. The Axis powers seemed unstoppable.

The Allies tried to hang on until their newest member was ready to help. U.S. military units swelled with new recruits, who needed training. Factories that made everyday items like cars and refrigerators had to retool. Their assembly lines would start making tanks and rifles. America was gearing up for war, but it wouldn't be ready overnight.

In the meantime, President Roosevelt decided the American people could use some good news. He ordered an air raid on Japan's home

Franklin D. Roosevelt (1882–1945) was first elected president in 1932. He guided America through the Great Depression and World War II. Roosevelt suffered from a paralyzing illness called polio. He could not walk, but it never stopped him from being a dynamic leader.

islands. The raid would be very small, nothing like the attack on Pearl Harbor. Instead this raid would be symbolic. It would show everyone that America was eager to fight.

Doolittle Raid

In April 1942, the aircraft carrier USS *Hornet* steamed through the Pacific. Sixteen B-25 bombers sat crammed on its deck. These large planes normally didn't serve aboard an aircraft carrier, but they were on a special mission. Once *Hornet* took them close enough to Japan, the bombers would raid the capital city of Tokyo.

An officer named Jimmy Doolittle led the bomber crews. Doolittle and his men were daring aviators, but even they worried about their secret mission. They would be flying deep into enemy territory, so the odds of being shot down were great. And while the bombers could take off from *Hornet*, they were far too big to land on the carrier. The raiders would need to land in China, which was also at war with Japan, and hope the Chinese could get them home.

One of sixteen B-25 bombers takes off from the deck of the USS Hornet, *on its way to take part in the first U.S. air raid on Japan. Although the Doolittle raid in April 1942 did not cause much damage to Tokyo, it did boost American confidence.*

The B-25 Mitchell bomber was named after General Billy Mitchell, the father of the U.S. Air Force. Mitchell foresaw war with Japan seventeen years before it actually happened. In fact, he predicted the war would begin with a surprise attack on Pearl Harbor.

One morning in Tokyo, residents gazed up to see warplanes flying overhead. They were accustomed to seeing Japanese aircraft, but the big planes overhead looked different. Their curiosity quickly turned to shock when the strange planes began dropping bombs. The explosions did only minor damage to the city, but the Japanese people were shaken. The once-distant war had come to their homeland.

Doolittle's raiders zoomed toward China. Before they could land, their planes sputtered and ran out of fuel. Most of the raiders managed to parachute to safety, including Jimmy Doolittle. Their exploits boosted America's spirits. Suddenly Japan no longer seemed so invincible. The raid worked just as President Roosevelt intended.

TEXT-DEPENDENT QUESTIONS

1. Prior to the attack on Pearl Harbor, what was America's attitude toward the war?

2. Which three nations were the original Allies?

3. What was the purpose of the Doolittle Raid?

RESEARCH PROJECT

A sailor named Dorie Miller earned the Navy Cross for his bravery at Pearl Harbor. Go to http://www.nationalgeographic.com/pearlharbor/ngbeyond/people/ and read his remarkable story. Then write three questions you would ask Dorie if he were alive today.

Chapter 2:

SEEDS OF WAR

In the late 1930s, the Axis powers posed a serious threat to freedom. Germany, Italy, and Japan were invading other nations. For the millions of Americans entering military service after the Pearl Harbor attack, their mission was clear. They needed to stop the Axis before it was too late. What was less obvious was how this crisis began. The Axis countries were home to ancient and respected cultures. Their citizens hoped for the same things as everyone else: happiness, health, good friends, and a loving family. Yet these same people also supported leaders who wanted to conquer neighbors and build empires. It made no sense.

WORDS TO UNDERSTAND IN THIS CHAPTER

coup—a sudden change of government, made illegally or by force.

propaganda—biased information used to sway public opinion.

treason—the crime of betraying one's own country.

The seeds of World War II had been sown decades earlier. They sprouted during the 1920s, and then bloomed in the 1930s. All three Axis nations underwent powerful changes during those years that would eventually lead to World War II.

Rise of the Fascists

In 1919, an Italian newspaper editor hunched over his desk. His name was Benito Mussolini. The First World War had just ended. Mussolini served in the Italian army during the war. In fact, he had been wounded. Now he was a civilian and a journalist again.

Mussolini grasped the power of the written word. He knew his articles influenced people. He was also an inspiring public speaker. His emotional arguments masked the fact that he twisted the truth. In other words, Mussolini was a master of *propaganda*. He told his fellow Italians that he wanted to return Italy to great glory, such as in the ancient days of the Roman Empire. The message intrigued his readers and listeners, especially young men. Soon he had many followers.

Mussolini organized his young followers into army-like units called *fasci*. The Fascists marched around in black uniforms. They did not hesitate to use violence. Anyone who openly disagreed with Mussolini could expect a visit from his thugs.

By 1922, eager Fascists bullied people throughout Italy. A black-shirted army paraded into Rome, the capital city. They demanded that Mussolini

With a raised fist, Benito Mussolini addresses supporters during a rally in Rome. The Italian leader often promised to return Italy to the glorious days of the Roman Empire.

become prime minister. The shaken Italian king agreed. Mussolini now had control over Italy's government. He began carrying out his plans for Italian glory.

Hitler Rises to Power

A 33-year-old German man was following the events in Italy with keen interest. His name was Adolf Hitler, and he had much in common with Mussolini. Hitler was a war veteran who had political ambition, just like Mussolini. He was also a gifted writer and speaker.

Memories of the First World War angered Hitler. He seethed about Germany's defeat, and the tough penalties that were imposed by the victors, including France and Britain. Germany had to disband its army and navy, and pay huge fines that crippled its economy. Hitler vowed to once again make Germany a world power. He became part of an organization of people who felt the same way, who called themselves National Socialists,

Hitler's failed coup actually helped the Nazi cause. The dramatic trial that followed turned him into a national celebrity. During his nine months in prison, Hitler wrote *Mein Kampf (My Struggle)*. The book promoted Nazi ideals, and became a bestseller in Germany.

or Nazis. Hitler soon became a Nazi leader, and began a propaganda campaign, borrowing many of Mussolini's methods.

In 1923, Hitler attempted a **coup** against the German government in Munich. It was too soon. He did not yet have enough followers, and the coup failed. Hitler went to jail for **treason**. During his time in prison, Hitler developed a new strategy for seizing control of Germany. He would try to get power by winning elections, rather than by force.

The Nazis added an element of hate to their propaganda. Hitler disliked Jewish people, so he cast them as the enemy. He claimed that Jewish politicians had caused Germany to lose the First World War. He also blamed Jewish bankers for Germany's economic woes. Hitler tried to unite German citizens by giving them an enemy to hate. At first, few people fell for his lies and half-truths. However, as the years of poverty and strife continued, they began to listen. Nazi beliefs slowly took root and spread.

A decade after his coup attempt, Hitler finally gained control of the German government. He became chancellor in 1933. His first task was to put people back to work. He created jobs by building roads, dams, and railways. Hitler also started building up the German army, navy, and air force. Workers were busy earning wages again. A revived Germany surged forward.

The military buildup violated an international treaty. Hitler didn't care. Other countries complained, but did little to stop what Germany was doing. They feared another conflict. Meanwhile, Hitler and Mussolini forged a treaty of their own, agreeing to support each other in the event of war. Nobody wanted to admit it, but Europe was once again sliding toward conflict.

After his arrest, Hitler sought to gain power through elections. This text of this propaganda poster claims that the National Socialists are making sacrifices to create a new Germany, and asks people to vote for the party in the 1932 election.

Japan Begins to Expand

On the other side of the planet, a new power had emerged. Until the 19th century, Japan had kept itself cut off from the rest of the world. Foreigners were banned, and few Japanese people ever left the home islands. That all changed in 1868, when a new emperor decided to modernize Japan. Emperor Meiji built factories, mills, schools, and shipyards. He hired foreigners to teach Japanese students the latest engineering and business practices. Meiji also cast aside the samurai warriors of the past in favor of a modern army and navy. By the end of his reign, Japan would be an economic and military powerhouse.

Japan's military soon had an opportunity to test its skills. In 1894, Japan went to war with China, and won easily. China gave up its claim to Korea, and handed over the island of Taiwan. A decade later, Japanese forces squared off against Russia. Again, the Japanese were victorious. Japan's military earned tremendous respect, both at home and abroad, for defeating the much-larger Russian Empire. The generals began looking for new conquests.

The international community condemned Japan's invasion of China in the mid-1930s, as well as many atrocities committed against Chinese civilians. This photo shows a crying Chinese baby in the bombed-out ruins of a Shanghai train station, 1937; the mother lies dead nearby.

They didn't need to search far. Japan's huge neighbor, China, once again made an easy target. China found it difficult to care for its far-flung citizens, much less protect its distant borders. During World War I, Japan fought on the side of France and Britain against Germany and its allies. They captured German territories in China, as well as Germany's Pacific island colonies. After the war ended, Japan tried to increase its control over China, which was experiencing political turmoil and a civil war.

Historians still argue today over Emperor Hirohito's role in the war. Some say he was merely a figurehead, leaving his generals to make all the decisions. Others believe Hirohito was closely involved, and should have faced charges as a war criminal.

In 1931, Japanese soldiers invaded the Chinese region called Manchuria. This brazen attack served as a wake-up call to other nations. Japan was building an empire.

At home, Japanese generals were slowly taking over the government. The emperor, Hirohito, did nothing to stop them. In fact, Hirohito often wore a uniform and carried a sword. Japanese citizens assumed he supported war and aggression. The generals fed the public a steady diet of wartime propaganda. The attack on China was justified, they said. Foreigners are inferior. Work hard. Be loyal to your emperor.

Before long, the nation fell under total military control. In 1936, Japan signed a pact with Germany. The Axis powers were now complete.

TEXT-DEPENDENT QUESTIONS

1. How did Mussolini become Italy's prime minister?
2. Why did Adolf Hitler go to prison?
3. Who was responsible for modernizing Japan?

RESEARCH PROJECT

The U.S. government also used propaganda during the war. Visit http://www.archives.gov/exhibits/powers_of_persuasion/powers_of_persuasion_home.html to see some American propaganda posters. Pick one and write a one-page report about why you think it is effective.

Chapter 3:

AXIS POWERS SURGE

World War II began in the predawn dark of September 1, 1939. German tanks, troops, and planes burst across the border into Poland. It would soon grow into the largest armed conflict in human history.

The attack on Poland did not come as a complete surprise. Germany had already taken over Austria and Czechoslovakia. When Hitler started eyeing Poland, the Polish army placed soldiers along its border. The

(Above) German troops parade through Warsaw, the capital of Poland, in the fall of 1939. The German army's use of tanks and dive bombers in coordination with motorized infantry enabled it to quickly conquer Poland and other European countries.

WORDS TO UNDERSTAND IN THIS CHAPTER

bunker—a covered shelter with openings for firing guns.

dictator—a ruler who has absolute control and power.

dogfighting—when fighter planes attempt to shoot each other down.

radar—a device that uses radio-wave echoes to locate objects.

soldiers dug in and waited, hoping the German attack would not come.

The leaders of France and Great Britain had hoped so, too. They desperately wished to avoid war, but Hitler was going too far. They warned him that an attack on Poland would not be tolerated. Hitler thought they were bluffing. After all, they had done little when he seized Austria and Czechoslovakia. He ordered the attack anyway. Two days after Germany's invasion, France and Great Britain declared war on Germany.

Lightning War

The Polish soldiers were heavily outnumbered. Even worse, their enemy was using a new attack style called *blitzkrieg*, or lightning war. Blitzkrieg relied on the latest advances in vehicle and airplane design to attack with incredible speed.

During the First World War, armies had advanced on foot. It was a slow, plodding style of warfare. Those days were over. In 1939, waves of German tanks and bombers dashed forward in unison. Truckloads of troops followed close behind. It all happened so quickly.

The Polish soldiers had planned to fight a grinding trench war, like in World War I. The German blitzkrieg overwhelmed them. Tens of thousands died. Within a week, the stunned survivors were desperately trying to defend their capital city of Warsaw.

Then came the final blow: an attack by the Soviet Union. Soviet troops poured into Poland from the east. They seized all the ground not yet captured by Germany. It turned out that Hitler and Soviet leader Josef Stalin had made a secret deal to divide Poland between Germany and the Soviet Union. After five weeks of crushing losses, Poland surrendered.

France under Siege

The swift victory in Poland proved that Germany's blitzkrieg tactics worked. Next, Hitler unleashed his armies against Western Europe. German troops pushed through the tiny neighbors of Belgium, Holland, and Luxembourg in May 1940. They set their sights on France, Germany's historic rival on the continent.

After World War I, France had built hundreds of concrete forts and bunkers along its border with Germany. These structures were intended to serve as a sturdy defense against invaders known as the Maginot Line. However, the soldiers who designed the Maginot Line had not imagined a mobile attack like blitzkrieg. In June 1940, fast-moving German forces simply bypassed the Maginot Line's forts and drove deep into France.

French and British soldiers fared no better than the Poles had against Hitler's finely tuned war

Adolf Hitler poses with several high-ranking Nazis in Paris after the fall of France, June 1940.

machine. They gave ground rapidly. This massive retreat finally ended on the beaches of the French port of Dunkirk. There was no place to go but into the water. German tanks and troops closed in for the kill.

British Prime Minister Winston Churchill organized a massive rescue. He sent every available ship to retrieve British soldiers stranded on the beaches of France. For nine days, more than 800 vessels, large and small, crisscrossed the English Channel, carrying shivering soldiers to safety. The Dunkirk evacuation saved 340,000 British troops from death or capture.

Despite this small bright spot, France was lost. A triumphant Hitler rode through Paris. Great Britain now stood isolated and alone. Only the English Channel saved it from the German blitzkrieg.

Battle of Britain

Hitler wanted to load his troops onto ships and send them across the English Channel. But in order to do that, he needed to knock out Britain's Royal Air Force. In July of 1940, planes of the German air force launched their assault. German fighters sought to shoot down British planes. Bombers targeted London, as well as factories and shipyards throughout Great Britain.

British pilots fought back with great skill and courage. They also had the advantage of *radar*, which warned them when German air attacks were coming. As alarms blared, the pilots would dash to their planes and take off. They engaged the attackers in aerial combat, known as *dogfighting*. The Battle of Britain raged in the sky for nearly four months.

British pilots shot down hundreds of German planes, but some bombers still got through. Nearly 40,000 London residents died during the

Winston Churchill (1874–1965) became British prime minister in 1940. Previously, he had been a soldier, author, and plucky politician. Churchill's speeches always inspired great hope and determination. He is remembered today as one of Britain's finest statesmen.

Children living in a suburb of London sit outside the wreckage of their home, which was destroyed by Nazi bombs during a nighttime raid in September 1940.

air raids. Survivors huddled in underground bomb shelters each night, waiting for the onslaught to end.

Finally, in November 1940, it did end. Hitler grew tired of the heavy aircraft losses. He scaled back the bombing raids and shelved his plans for an invasion of Britain. The Royal Air Force had won. Hitler consoled himself by choosing a new target. His next attack would be his biggest yet, and the victim would have no idea it was coming.

Operation Barbarossa

In 1939, Hitler and Soviet leader Josef Stalin had secretly agreed to invade Poland together. At that time, they also pledged never to attack each other. To formalize the deal, German and Soviet diplomats signed a non-aggression pact.

Stalin felt relieved. He had no desire to face the German war machine. The Soviet Union was a massive country. Even his huge Soviet army would struggle to defend its borders from a German blitzkrieg. Stalin watched as Nazi troops surged through Western Europe in 1940. He was grateful for the non-aggression pact. He had no clue that Hitler planned to break it.

In June 1941, Hitler let loose the largest invasion in history. He called it Operation Barbarossa, after an ancient German emperor. More than 3.7 million soldiers and 3,300 tanks poured into the Soviet Union. They swept through towns and cities, capturing hundreds of miles of territory. Hitler wanted a swift victory before the bitter Russian winter arrived. He urged his generals forward.

Josef Stalin was a *dictator*, and was no stranger to shrewd tricks. But Hitler's betrayal surprised even him. Stalin ordered a hasty counterattack, which failed miserably. Then he ordered the Soviet army to hold its ground at all costs. They did, and more than a million soldiers were killed or wounded. The Soviet defense was a disaster.

The summer wore on, and Hitler's generals pushed ever deeper into the Soviet Union. The German army smashed Soviet tanks, shot down planes, and captured enemy

This map shows, in red, the large area of Soviet territory captured by the German Army in the first two months of its invasion of the USSR.

The Soviet Union was an alliance of communist republics, led by Russia. It was a huge country, the largest in the world by area. The Soviet Union was dissolved in 1991, and broke into 15 independent nations.

soldiers. But Stalin refused to surrender. He just sent more troops into battle. He seemed to have an endless supply. The German generals continued their assault.

By the fall of 1941, Hitler ruled a new German empire that stretched covered nearly all of Europe. Italian and German troops held large portions of the North African desert. Japan continued its conquest of China and Southeast Asia. Then came the December 7 attack on Pearl Harbor. The Axis powers were on a global rampage, and it seemed nothing could stop their conquests.

TEXT-DEPENDENT QUESTIONS

1. What was *blitzkrieg*, and why was it so successful?
2. What forced Hitler to cancel his invasion of Great Britain?
3. Why was Josef Stalin so surprised by Germany's attack on his country?

RESEARCH PROJECT

For the first two years of the war, America stayed neutral, at least officially. Meanwhile, President Roosevelt did his best to help the Allies. Go to https://history.state.gov/milestones/1937-1945/lend-lease and learn about his Lend-Lease program. Make a list of basic weapons and supplies you think Great Britain probably needed to survive.

Chapter 4:

ALLIES FIGHT BACK

As 1942 began, the Allies weighed their options. They needed to strike back. The Axis powers had already captured so much territory. It was difficult to know where to start. Winston Churchill suggested North Africa. British soldiers were already slugging it out there with German and Italian troops. If the Allies could free North Africa, an attack on Europe would go easier. Churchill called North Africa the "soft underbelly" of the Axis.

(Above) Japanese planes fly through heavy fire to attack the American aircraft carrier USS Yorktown *during the Battle of Midway. Carrier-based aircraft would have a major impact on the Pacific theater of the war.*

WORDS TO UNDERSTAND IN THIS CHAPTER

armada—a fleet of warships.

convoy—a group of vehicles or ships traveling together.

mortar—a small cannon designed to throw shells at high angles.

reinforcements—an additional supply of troops, tanks, aircraft, and the like.

Franklin Roosevelt agreed. American soldiers boarded ships for North Africa. They would soon get their first taste of combat. And it would happen in the desert.

Meanwhile, the U.S. Navy got underway in the Pacific. Japanese warships roamed the vast ocean. Nobody knew where they might strike next. An American armada set out after them. These two powerful navies finally found each other off the coast of Australia, in the Coral Sea. The result was a first in military history.

Carriers Clash

Airplanes were already making a big impact in the war. At the Battle of the Coral Sea, they led the way. In fact, this was the first naval battle in history where the opposing ships never actually saw each other.

The battle began with planes from both sides flying almost blind in heavy fog. They searched for enemy aircraft carriers. The Americans struck first. Dive-bombers from the USS *Lexington* swooped in on the Japanese carrier *Soho*, sinking it in just ten minutes.

Next Japanese planes found the *Lexington*, and showered it with bombs and torpedoes. It too sank. Both sides lost other ships before withdrawing. Tactically, the five-day battle was a victory for Japan, as the Americans lost more ships. However, strategically it was a victory for the Allies. The sea battle prevented a Japanese invasion of Australia. It also proved that aircraft carriers were the dominant warships of the sea, even more important than mighty battleships.

The Coral Sea clash turned out to be a warm-up for an even bigger carrier battle. In June 1942, U.S. warplanes surprised a Japanese armada near the island of Midway. For two days, aircraft carriers from both sides launched vicious air attacks. When it was over, four Japanese carriers sat at the bottom of the ocean, while the U.S. Navy lost only one, USS *Yorktown*. The Allies had crippled the Japanese fleet, and won their first major victory in the Pacific.

This illustration depicts members of the U.S. 32nd Infantry Division fighting Japanese forces in the jungle of New Guinea during 1942.

Marines Move In

With Japan's navy still reeling from the Battle of Midway, U.S. Marines began their mission. The Marines were experts at seaborne landings. They planned to land on islands held by Japanese troops and capture them.

The Marines first assaulted an island called Guadalcanal. Landing craft carried them ashore, and they hurried past the beaches into thick jungle. Japanese defenders put up a fierce fight, but they were outnumbered. The Marines captured their primary target, a newly built airfield. It seemed like a quick victory, but then Japanese *reinforcements* arrived.

The battle for Guadalcanal lasted six ugly months. Men from both sides endured bloody combat, malnutrition, and jungle diseases. At last the Marines prevailed, but Guadalcanal taught them a tough lesson. There would be no quick victories in the Pacific.

Capturing every Japanese-held island would take forever. So the Marines, as well as U.S. Army troops that joined them, targeted only certain islands to attack. They focused on the ones with the greatest strategic value, and bypassed the rest. This "island hopping" plan would enable the U.S. military to leapfrog across the Pacific toward Japan.

Steel Sharks

American and Japanese submarines prowled the Pacific like steel sharks. These underwater predators searched for troop ships and other valuable targets.

Ship crews knew a sub attack might come at any time, and without warning. Torpedoes streaming toward their vessel would explode on contact,

Germany sent coded radio messages to its U-boats using a secret machine called Enigma. When British and Polish code-breakers learned how to decode the Enigma messages, it gave the Allies a huge advantage, as they knew in advance where to expect attacks.

A photo taken through the periscope of a U.S. submarine shows a torpedoed Japanese warship sinking in the Pacific, 1942.

ripping holes in the hull. Passengers hurried for lifeboats or dove into the water, and hoped for rescue. During the course of the war, subs sent thousands of ships to the dark depths of the Pacific.

In the Atlantic Ocean, German U-boats decimated Allied shipping. The U-boats hunted together in groups called "wolf packs." They were trying to stop the vital flow of weapons and supplies bound for Great Britain and the Soviet Union. In the early years of the war, they very nearly succeeded.

Ships began to travel in large *convoys* for safety. They sailed zigzag routes, but still the wolf packs found them. The Atlantic became a watery graveyard as more than 1,700 supply ships were lost to U-boat attacks.

By late 1942, the tide of war started turning against the wolf packs. American warships now protected the convoys. They carried depth charges to blast submarines out of the water. New long-range bombers patrolled the Atlantic, looking for dark shadows just below the surface.

The U-boats went from being hunters to the hunted. Nearly 700 were destroyed. With the U-boat threat gone, supply-laden ships could once again steam across the Atlantic, bringing war material to America's allies.

Showdown at Stalingrad

In Russia, the German attack stalled during the winter of 1941–42. Hitler's armies kept pounding their way toward Moscow, the Soviet capital. In 1942 they captured valuable Soviet oil fields. But so far, complete victory eluded them.

In the summer of 1942, Hitler decided on a new strategy. He told his generals to attack the city of Stalingrad. It was an odd choice. The generals knew the key to victory was Moscow, not Stalingrad. They pleaded with Hitler to reconsider, but he refused. He thought Germany could destroy the Soviet army there before another cold winter set in. The massive German invasion force changed course. It started moving toward Stalingrad.

Soviet dictator Josef Stalin decided to hold at the city at all cost. He ordered every man, woman, and child to mount a defense. An epic showdown was brewing. The struggle for Stalingrad would become the largest and bloodiest battle in the history of warfare.

German planes first bombed the city to soften its defenses. Then the tanks and troops arrived, and began pushing through the streets. Stalingrad's defenders gave fierce resistance. They worked in small groups, and fought to hold every street corner and building. Snipers from both sides crouched inside smoldering ruins. Corpses lay everywhere.

One Stalingrad factory kept producing tanks even as combat raged all around it. When German troops breached its walls, workers stopped to help repel them, then went back to work. New tanks rolled straight out of the factory and into battle.

This painting by a Soviet artist shows a Russian army preparing to cross the Volga River and engage the invading Germans at Stalingrad.

Soviet women fought as snipers, machine gunners, and **mortar** operators. Nobody was exempt from service. Stalin reinforced the city with men and women from all over the country. Many of these newcomers carried no weapons. If they couldn't find a rifle on the ground, they had to wait for one to become available. They rarely had to wait long, as thousands of soldiers were dying every day.

By November 1942, German forces held 90 percent of the city. Snow had begun to fall. The Germans grew obsessed with finishing off Stalingrad before winter. They failed to notice some movement on the outskirts of the city. Quietly, fresh Soviet troops were massing for a counterattack.

Hitler had ignored his generals when they urged against an attack on Stalingrad. He ignored them often. Hitler considered himself a brilliant strategist. Soon he would learn the results of his arrogance.

 # TEXT-DEPENDENT QUESTIONS

1. Why was the naval battle at the Coral Sea unique?
2. What did U.S. Marines learn at Guadalcanal?
3. What was a group of German U-boats called?

 # RESEARCH PROJECT

Many American women served in war zones overseas. Many more worked long hours in shipyards and arms factories at home. Do some research on "Rosie the Riveter" and write a one-page essay about her. Be sure to list your sources.

Chapter 5:

TURNING POINT

German troops thought victory was near at Stalingrad. In reality, they verged on a crushing defeat. Josef Stalin was preparing a huge counterstrike to drive them from his prized city.

Stalin's million-man attack succeeded in less than a day. As Soviet artillery roared, his tanks and troops launched their own blitzkrieg. They avoided a frontline assault, instead slashing at the German flanks, or sides, where the defenses were weaker.

Soviet forces broke through the flanks. They raced 40 miles behind the lines and surrounded the German troops. Hitler's generals were horrified.

(Above) A U.S. Navy combat artist produced this illustration of the battle for a section of Omaha Beach, Normandy. The D-Day landing on the French coast was the largest amphibious assault in history, involving more than 150,000 soldiers, most of whom were American, British, or Canadian.

WORDS TO UNDERSTAND IN THIS CHAPTER

atoll—a ring-shaped coral island or chain of islands.

landing craft—a flat-bottomed boat for taking troops and equipment close to shore.

paratrooper—a soldier trained to parachute from airplanes.

siege—surrounding and attacking a fortified place, so that it cannot receive help or supplies.

The army needed to retreat immediately, or it would become trapped at Stalingrad.

Hitler told them he would not permit a retreat. They would stay and fight, he said. He promised to send airplanes with fresh supplies. Hitler's foolish order doomed the German soldiers trapped at Stalingrad. They were outnumbered nearly five to one. The combat grew more vicious than ever. Their food and ammunition ran low. Supply planes brought more, but not nearly enough. Many people froze to death.

By February 1943, the 100,000 Germans still alive at Stalingrad surrendered. It was a turning point for Hitler's war machine. He had wasted too many lives and weapons on the siege of Stalingrad. From now on, Germany would be fighting a defensive war.

Italy Switches Sides

As the drama unfolded in Russia, soldiers from the United States and Britain set to work in North Africa. The Americans were new to combat, and it showed. They lost battles against veteran German troops, who were led by General Erwin Rommel, nicknamed the "Desert Fox."

With each defeat, however, the Americans gained more experience. They also got a new leader, General George Patton, who instilled discipline and confidence in his tank crews. Soon the Allies chased Rommel and his troops from North Africa.

The next step was an Allied invasion of Italy, which began in July 1943. By this point, Italians had grown tired of the war. Mussolini was a great speechmaker, but a poor wartime leader. He had promised them glory, but all he had delivered was misery and defeat. Even Mussolini's loyal followers, the Fascists, lost faith in him. They demanded that he step down as prime minister.

With Mussolini gone, the Italian government switched sides and joined the Allies. It was more bad news for Hitler. He sent German troops to seize control of Rome. Now, German forces were tied down defending Italy as well.

Terror at Tarawa

In the Pacific, America's island-hopping campaign continued. Soldiers and Marines plodded across the ocean toward Japan. Each new island promised a savage struggle. Japanese troops were always dug in and waiting.

In November 1943, thousands of U.S. Marines clambered down from their transport ships into small *landing craft*. They would be going ashore on Tarawa *Atoll* in the Gilbert Islands. The Marines squinted through sea spray as they approached. U.S. airplanes and naval guns peppered the two-mile island. The assault was going according to plan.

Then trouble began. The landing craft became snagged on coral reefs just below the surface. They were stuck. Japanese artillery and machine

Prior to D-Day, the Allies used decoys to mask their true invasion plans. They set out inflatable tanks, airplanes, and landing craft, which looked real to German scout planes. Fake radio messages by this "ghost army" added to the deception. Because of this, the Germans believed that the attack would come at the French port of Calais. They moved soldiers there from Normandy.

U.S. Marines storm Tarawa, an atoll in the Gilbert Islands.

guns opened up. The Marines climbed over the side and splashed into the water. Their weapons and equipment were heavy, making it hard not to drown. Explosions and bullets tore into the water as they struggled for shore. Many never made it.

The Battle of Tarawa pushed both sides to their limits. Waves of Marines stubbornly fought their way up the beach. Japanese troops, meanwhile, poured down fire. They vowed to die fighting rather than surrender the little island.

In the end, Tarawa's 4,500 defenders kept their pledge. After four days of brutal combat, all but seventeen were dead. The Marines captured the island, but it cost them more than 3,000 dead or wounded of their own.

Gearing Up for D-Day

Hitler was spreading his forces too thin. The enormous Soviet conflict constantly required new tanks, troops, and supplies. In Italy, German soldiers fought to hold back advancing British and American forces. And now Germany herself was under attack from the sky. Long-range U.S. bombers flew raids from England every night, seeking to destroy German arms factories. Hitler's finely tuned war machine began to sputter. The Allies decided it was time to take back France.

Putting troops on the French coast would be risky. German soldiers had already spent years building strong beach defenses. They nestled concrete bunkers in jagged cliffs overlooking the shore. On the sand below, they buried mines and built obstacles. German machine guns and artillery were pointed at every square inch of beach. Hitler boasted that his coastal defenses formed an impenetrable "Atlantic Wall."

An American general, Dwight Eisenhower, planned the invasion of France. Eisenhower would someday become U.S. president, but right now he faced the toughest challenge of his military career. He needed to crack Hitler's Atlantic Wall. Eisenhower and his planners referred to the invasion date, which was not yet set, as D-Day.

By early 1944, England teemed with troops, vehicles, aircraft, and ships. Soldiers practiced seaborne landings, but the location of their actual attack remained a mystery. The soldiers tried to guess where they were going. Hitler was guessing too, which is exactly what Eisenhower wanted.

June 6, 1944

Eisenhower and his staff chose the Normandy region of France. The attack would involve more than 150,000 troops, making it the largest seaborne

American soldiers leave their landing craft under heavy German machine-gun fire, heading for the beach at Normandy, June 6, 1944.

invasion in history. Bad weather postponed it for a day. The new date was June 6, 1944.

American and British *paratroopers* went in first. Hundreds of transport planes carried them to France long before daybreak. They parachuted into Normandy, well behind the Atlantic Wall. Their job was to seize key bridges and roads, so the Germans could not rush reinforcements to the beaches.

From the English Channel, an armada of Allied warships opened fire. Airplanes joined the bombardment. They targeted a 50-mile stretch of coastline where American, British, and Canadian troops would land. The Normandy beaches were given codenames: Utah, Omaha, Gold, Juno, and Sword.

The first wave of landing craft arrived at dawn. Cold wind produced choppy waves that made the soldiers seasick. As the landing craft drew closer, bullets rattled against their steel hulls. Then the front gates fell open, and thousands of soldiers were splashing through frigid water. Machine guns cut down dozens in the first few seconds.

The killing was worst at Omaha beach. German fire rained from the hills as American soldiers struggled ashore. Combat engineers tried to clear away barbed wire and other obstacles. Explosions and bullets sprayed sand into the air. Men crawled into bomb craters for cover, but their officers urged them forward. The only way to survive was to get off the beach.

By mid-morning, small groups were working their way up the hillside paths toward German bunkers. Landing craft continued to bring reinforcements. By afternoon all the beaches were open. Troops and

Early reports of the carnage at Omaha beach led Hitler to believe the Allies had failed, so he held back his best troops. By the time he learned the truth, it was too late.

tanks began moving inland, where they found more German defenses. Much fighting still remained, but D-Day was a success. The Allies had gained a toehold in France. They would soon start working their way toward Germany.

TEXT-DEPENDENT QUESTIONS

1. How did the Soviets win at Stalingrad?
2. Why did Mussolini lose control of Italy?
3. What was the Atlantic Wall?

RESEARCH PROJECT

Imagine you are General Dwight Eisenhower visiting with your troops before D-Day. These men will soon be risking their lives in battle. Write a one-page speech of encouragement. For guidance, listen to Eisenhower's actual D-Day message at http://www.army.mil/d-day/history.html?from=dday_rotator_eisenhower#video

Chapter 6:

CIVILIANS SUFFER

World War II was the worst conflict in history. At least 55 million people died. More than half of those victims did not serve in any military. They were unarmed civilians.

Some of the men, women, and children who died were killed accidentally. Many others were intentionally targeted, either because of who they were or where they lived.

(Above) American B-24 bombers conduct an aerial raid on a German facility. Both the Axis and Allied powers engaged in strategic bombing campaigns that targeted enemy cities and killed millions of civilians.

WORDS TO UNDERSTAND IN THIS CHAPTER

ethnic—pertaining to people who have the same national background, culture, religion, and language.

Holocaust—originally meaning a devastating fire, this word now refers to Hitler's mass slaughter of Jewish people.

partisan—a person who takes up arms to fight an occupying army.

sabotage—to destroy or disrupt normal operations, such as by planting a bomb.

Strategic Bombing

Both sides engaged in strategic bombing of cities. Newly designed aircraft made massive bombing raids possible. Formations of large, powerful planes appeared over cities. During a single raid, they could drop thousands of high-explosive and incendiary (fire-producing) bombs. The result was devastating.

Bombers sought to destroy factories—and their civilian workers—in order to cripple an enemy's war-making ability. Valuable targets included weapons factories, oil refineries, and aircraft plants. But the planes had a second mission: to scare and dishearten city residents. Bombs flattened entire neighborhoods. The idea was to crush an enemy's will to fight.

The Axis powers used strategic bombing during their years of aggression. Japanese bombers first attacked Chinese cities in 1937. Germany's bombers ravaged Polish cities during the 1939 invasion that triggered the war in Europe. The following year, German bombers killed more than 40,000 British civilians before the Royal Air Force finally defeated them.

Later in the war, American and British planes took strategic bombing to horrifying new levels. Allied bombing raids on the German city of Hamburg killed 42,000 civilians in a single week. In the Pacific, U.S.

bombers repeatedly struck Japanese cities in 1944 and 1945. More than 330,000 civilians died during these terrifying raids.

The strategic bombing of cities during World War II remains a controversial issue even today. Critics say the intentional attacks on civilians were immoral. Supporters argue that the bombings helped end the war, saving lives.

Crimes against Humanity

For years, propaganda in Japan and Germany portrayed foreigners as subhuman. Foreign lives held no value, the propaganda said. Soldiers who had been brainwashed with this notion since childhood accepted it as fact.

When they invaded other countries, Japanese and German troops often showed little regard for the people living there. The soldiers committed brutal crimes against humanity. These acts had nothing to do with winning the war. They were perpetrated far from the front lines, against people who were non-combatants.

In December 1937, Japan's army captured the Chinese city of Nanjing. For six weeks, Japanese soldiers went on a killing spree of city residents. The soldiers raped thousands of women and young girls before murdering them. Nobody knows for certain how many civilians perished in the Nanjing Massacre. Estimates range from 40,000 to more than 300,000.

German forces used terror to control people in the nations they occupied. A fanatical Nazi military group called the *Schutzstaffel*, or S.S., enforced strict order. Tools of the S.S. included kidnapping, torture, and execution.

Hitler was obsessed with race. He envisioned a world of white people, particularly those with blond hair and blue eyes. Hitler sought to eliminate anyone who didn't fit into his racial purity plans, especially Jewish people.

Countless individuals were taken from their homes in the middle of the night, and never seen again.

Harsh S.S. tactics were not entirely effective, and in some cases actually spurred people to fight back. Many Nazi-occupied countries had secret resistance movements. These *partisans* helped the Allies by spying on German troops and conducting *sabotage*. On several occasions, the S.S. retaliated by rounding up and executing random groups of civilians.

The Holocaust

Adolf Hitler committed an atrocity so vast and evil that it almost defies description. He attempted genocide, the mass killing of a nationality or *ethnic* group. Hitler's war against Jews, and other people he found undesirable, resulted in millions of deaths. Estimates of those killed during

German SS officers sort Jewish prisoners, who have just arrived by train, on the railway platform outside the notorious Auschwitz-Birkenau concentration camp in Poland. Healthy Jews were forced to work in nearby factories; the old and sick were executed in gas chambers within hours of their arrival.

the *Holocaust* range from 11 million men, women, and children, to as many as 20 million.

Hitler began persecuting German Jews soon after he came to power in 1933. He took away their citizenship and their jobs, and forbade them from attending school. Many Jewish people fled Germany. Jews who didn't leave ended up in slave labor camps, called concentration camps. Homosexuals, political prisoners, and others that Hitler disliked were sent to these camps also.

Life in the concentration camps was unbearable. Prisoners received little food and no medical care. They worked nonstop in the cold. Many starved, froze, or became ill. S.S. guards killed anyone who grew too weak to work. Nazi doctors performed gruesome medical experiments. More than a hundred concentration camps would spring up across Europe.

When the war began in 1939, Hitler set up mobile killing units called Action Groups. After the German army captured new territory, these S.S. units swept in to gather all Jewish people from the towns and villages. The Action Groups took their prisoners into the woods and machine-gunned them. During their first year in the Soviet Union, the Action Groups murdered half a million men, women, and children.

Hitler's "Final Solution"

Concentration camps and mobile killing squads were not enough for Hitler. He wanted a more efficient method. His Final Solution involved enormous death camps, each one capable of killing thousands of people every day.

Prisoners arrived at the death camps after being stuffed inside railway freight cars. They did not know the camp's true purpose. Guards ordered them to strip off their clothes for a shower, and then herded them into a gigantic chamber. Once everyone was inside, the guards locked the doors.

After a moment the shower began. But instead of spraying water, pipes overhead spewed poison gas. Twenty minutes later, all the prisoners were dead. Corpses were looted of jewelry and any gold tooth-fillings.

S.S. guards used other prisoners for this ghoulish job, falsely promising that they would be spared.

The gas chambers were so efficient that the S.S. had trouble with corpse disposal. Bodies could not be buried fast enough, so they were burned. Some camps used special ovens, which ran around the clock to keep up. The largest camp, Auschwitz-Birkenau, could dispose of 4,400 bodies per day.

By late 1944, Germany was losing the war. Hitler's forces labored to hold off the Soviets in Eastern Europe, and the Americans and British soldiers advancing through Western Europe. Yet Hitler still devoted troops to rounding up and killing Jews.

Before long, Allied armies began pushing into Nazi territory containing death camps. Heinrich Himmler, chief of the S.S., saw a problem. If Germany were defeated, the victors would surely punish those responsible

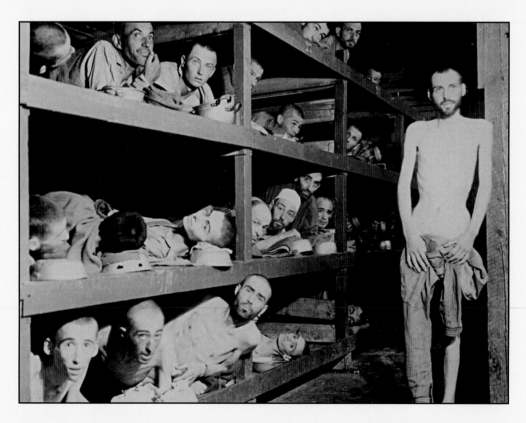

These Jewish slave laborers, suffering from malnutrition and disease, were freed when U.S. troops liberated the concentration camp at Buchenwald in April 1945.

Germany was not the only country that put people in detention camps. After Pearl Harbor, the U.S. government removed 110,000 Japanese Americans from their West Coast homes due to fears they might be loyal to Japan. They spent more than two years under guard in crowded camps. The U.S. government eventually admitted that the internment of Japanese Americans had been unjust, and in 1988 awarded a payment of $20,000 to all those still living who had been held in the detention camps. Here, Japanese-American women stand outside a building at the detention camp at Tule Lake, California.

for the death camps, including Himmler himself. The Final Solution, he realized, needed to remain a secret. Himmler closed and dismantled any death camp at risk of being captured. The rest continued their heinous work.

 ## TEXT-DEPENDENT QUESTIONS

1. Why is strategic bombing a controversial topic?
2. What did German and Japanese propaganda say about foreigners?
3. What was the Final Solution?

 ## RESEARCH PROJECT

America's minorities played important roles in winning the war, despite shabby treatment by the U.S. government and society at large. Research the Tuskegee Airmen and the 100th Infantry Battalion. Write a paragraph about each, describing their efforts. Be sure to list your sources.

Chapter 7:

BITTER END, NEW BEGINNING

By December 1944, Germany was in serious trouble. Hitler's troops fought stubbornly, but their enemy was too strong. Slowly, they yielded most of the territory captured earlier in the war. Meanwhile, Allied bombers turned German cities to rubble.

Hitler planned one final gamble. He wanted to unleash a huge blitzkrieg-style attack against the Americans and British. His generals listened with unease. The days of blitzkrieg were over. They needed every last soldier to

(Above) American soldiers fight in the Ardennes Forest during the Battle of the Bulge. The German offensive in December 1944 took the Allies by surprise, but it was soon halted and by the end of January 1945 American troops were continuing their march toward Berlin, the German capital.

WORDS TO UNDERSTAND IN THIS CHAPTER

casualties—troops who are killed, wounded, or captured.

nuclear fission—splitting the nucleus of an atom into nuclei
of lighter atoms, which produces a release of energy.

defend the homeland. If this gamble failed, Germany would be doomed. Hitler ignored their concerns. As always, he brimmed with overconfidence.

His plan was daring. More than 200,000 German troops and 350 tanks would burst through the center of the Allied lines. They would split the American and British forces in half. Hitler swept his hand triumphantly across the map. He said his blitzkrieg would thrust all the way to the port city of Antwerp, Belgium. He then pointed to the spot where the attack would begin: the Ardennes Forest.

Battle of the Bulge

The Ardennes Forest is a thick knot of hills, trees, rivers, and boulders. In winter, waist-deep snow makes it virtually impassable. General Dwight Eisenhower deemed this area the safest in his line. The units he left guarding it were either inexperienced or exhausted from previous battles.

The Ardennes suddenly came alive on December 16, 1944. A German artillery barrage opened the battle. Dazed American soldiers could scarcely believe their eyes. Enemy troops and tanks were emerging, ghost-like, along a 50-mile stretch of forest.

The Americans fell back. Eisenhower sent reinforcements, but they would take time to arrive. Heavy fog kept Allied airplanes on the ground. They couldn't help the frontline troops. Newspaper reporters studied their maps, and saw that the German assault was creating a salient, or C-shaped bulge, in the American lines. The next morning, people all across the United States read frantic headlines about the Battle of the Bulge.

Hitler poured more troops and tanks into the Bulge. They slashed deeper into Belgium, still sheltered from air attacks by bad weather. American paratroopers dug in at the crossroads town of Bastogne. German forces surrounded Bastogne and began laying siege. The paratroopers' food and ammunition ran low but for days they held on, fending off constant attacks.

After one tense week, the weather finally cleared. Allied airplanes took to the skies and quickly halted the German advance. On the ground, reinforcements began the arduous task of shrinking the Bulge. A month later it was gone, and the surviving German troops were back in their original lines. Hitler's final gamble had failed. An invasion of Germany was now inevitable.

Japan's Suicide Attacks

In the Pacific, America's island-hopping strategy was paying off. Each hard-won victory gave the Americans islands where they could build runways for airplanes. This brought U.S. long-range bombers closer to Japan. At home, war production reached full power. New vessels sailed from U.S. shipyards daily. Aircraft plants, meanwhile, produced 8,000 new warplanes each month. Japan's war industry simply could not keep up.

Japanese forces used every possible method to halt the American advance, including suicide attacks. When an island was about to be lost, the remaining Japanese soldiers would mount a final desperate assault. Screaming *"Tenno heika banzai!"* ("Long live the emperor!"), they would charge forward, hoping to overwhelm the American soldiers. Few banzai charges succeeded, but they did inflict heavy *casualties*.

Not all Germans believed in Hitler. In fact, during the war more than a dozen attempts were made on his life. In July 1944, a group of German officers planted a bomb under his map table. Hitler was injured, but survived. The officers were executed.

Fire blazes on the USS Bunker Hill *after two kamakaze planes hit the carrier simultaneously off the Japanese island of Kyushu, May 1945. The attack killed nearly 350 American sailors and wounded over 260 others.*

Suicide attacks from the air were flown by *kamikaze* (divine wind) pilots. This tactic first appeared in late 1944. Kamikaze pilots chose a high-value target, such as an aircraft carrier, and flew straight for it. They ignored the fighters and anti-aircraft guns trying to shoot them down. Their only goal was to survive long enough to crash into their target. One in five succeeded, and dozens of U.S. warships sank after being hit by kamikazes.

By early 1945, American generals and admirals were contemplating an invasion of the Japanese home islands. It was a distressing thought. Japanese troops had already proved they would die fighting rather than surrender. The defense of their home islands would be the fiercest yet.

Plus, the Japanese government was training civilians to use rifles, grenades, and suicide bombs.

During the invasion, military planners expected that American forces could expect to suffer casualties as high as one million. Japanese dead and wounded would be even higher. Yet the generals and admirals proceeded with their plans. They could not risk leaving Japan intact, to rebuild and possibly threaten the Pacific once more. The invasion was scheduled for November 1945.

Victory in Europe

Time was running out for Hitler. Only a sliver of his once mighty war machine remained, and the Allies were crushing it with a vise-like attack. Soviet forces advanced from the east, while American and British armies pressed from the west.

The broad Rhine River blocked the Allied path into western Germany. Hitler ordered all of its bridges destroyed, but U.S. forces managed to capture a railroad bridge intact. Tanks and troops flowed across it. To the east, Josef Stalin assembled his largest army yet, with a goal of overrunning the German capital of Berlin.

In April 1945, Italian partisans caught former dictator Benito Mussolini as he tried to escape to Switzerland. They executed him. Meanwhile, Hitler hid in an underground bunker as the Battle of Berlin raged overhead. When it became obvious the end was near, Hitler and other high-ranking Nazis committed suicide.

Leaders of the new German government surrendered, and its people began the hard work of rebuilding their war-torn lives. They discovered that defeat meant the division of their country. The Soviet Union soon established East Germany as a communist state under its control. Meanwhile, a democratic West Germany quickly recovered with U.S. help, and prospered. In 1990, as the Soviet Union collapsed, East and West Germany reunited into a single nation.

The Atomic Era

In the early 1940s, during the war's darkest hours, President Franklin Roosevelt had authorized the top-secret Manhattan Project. Thousands of scientists hurried to develop the world's first atomic bomb. In July 1945, they succeeded in building an atomic weapon that would be far more powerful than traditional bombs. It released tremendous energy by splitting atoms, a process called *nuclear fission*. A test explosion in the New Mexico desert proved its remarkable destructive force. The scientists reported their bomb ready.

A dense column of smoke rises over the Japanese port of Nagasaki after an atomic bomb was dropped on the city on August 9, 1945. This devastating weapon, as well as a Soviet declaration of war on Japan, led the Japanese emperor to surrender to the Allies, ending the Second World War.

Representatives of the Japanese government board the USS Missouri *to sign the formal surrender document in Tokyo harbor, September 1945.*

Roosevelt had died in office a few months earlier. The new president, Harry Truman, faced a tough decision—whether to use this devastating new weapon against Japan. Truman knew the bomb would kill many Japanese civilians. He also thought about the Americans who would die if Japan's home islands were invaded. He decided to use the atomic bomb.

On August 6, 1945, an American B-29 appeared high over the city of Hiroshima. It released a single bomb. A tremendous blast and firestorm followed, which leveled 70 percent of the city. More than 70,000 people died. Three days later, another atomic bomb hit the city of Nagasaki, with similar results. At last, Japan surrendered. After six long years, World War II was finally over.

American troops, led by General Douglas MacArthur, occupied Japan for the next six years. During that time, MacArthur introduced many democratic reforms to Japanese society. Postwar Japan thrived economically, and became a key ally of the United States.

After the war, the Allies conducted military trials in Nuremberg, Germany. Nazis found guilty of the Holocaust and other atrocities were either hanged or sent to prison. Similar trials took place in Tokyo for Japanese war criminals.

TEXT-DEPENDENT QUESTIONS

1. How did the Battle of the Bulge get its name?
2. What was a banzai charge?
3. What new weapon forced Japan's surrender?

RESEARCH PROJECT

The United Nations, or U.N., formed in 1945 with the goal of preventing another world war. Ambassadors from around the world meet to discuss international problems. Research the U.N. to find out why some people praise it and others criticize it. Write a one-page paper describing your own opinion about the U.N.

CHRONOLOGY

1931   In September, Japan invades the Chinese province of Manchuria.

1933   Adolf Hitler is elected chancellor of Germany.

1935   Benito Mussolini sends Italian soldiers to conquer Ethiopia.

1936   Germany signs treaties with Italy and Japan.

1937   Japan invades China, initiating war in the Pacific.

1938   Germany annexes neighboring Austria, and seizes territory in Czechoslovakia.

1939   Germany and the Soviet Union sign an agreement that they will not fight each other, and secretly agree to conquer and divide Poland. On September 1, Germany invades Poland. Two days later, France and Great Britain declare war on Germany, starting World War II in Europe.

1940   Germany invades and conquers Denmark, Norway, Luxembourg, the Netherlands, Belgium, and France. The German air force bombs British cities in preparation for an invasion, but is repulsed in the Battle of Britain. The Soviet Union occupies the Balkan Peninsula and southeastern Europe. Italy invades British territory in Egypt. In September,

Germany, Italy, and Japan sign the Tripartite Pact, creating the Axis powers.

1941   Germany soldiers are sent to help the Italians fight the British in North Africa. Gemany and its allies capture Yugoslavia and Greece. In June, Germany launches an invasion of the Soviet Union, reaching the outskirts of Moscow by October. On

December 7, the Japanese launch a surprise attack of the U.S. military base at Pearl Harbor. The next day, the United States declares war on Japan, entering World War II.

1942 Japanese troops capture the Philippines, French Indochina, and British Singapore. In June, the U.S. and British navies halt the Japanese advance at the Battle of Midway. Germany launches a new offensive in the Soviet Union, reaching the city of Stalingrad. In November, U.S. and British troops land in North Africa to fight the Germans and Italians.

1943 The German Sixth Army is trapped in Stalingrad and surrenders in February. After months of fighting, U.S. Marines finally drive the Japanese garrison from Guadalcanal. The Allies gain control of North Africa, capture Sicily, and land troops in southern Italy.

1944 Allied troops liberate Rome. On D-Day (June 6), Allied troops land on the beaches of Normandy and begin the task of driving the German Army out of France. The Soviet Union launches a massive offensive and recaptures most of the territory lost in 1941. In the Pacific, U.S. troops land on the Philippines in October, and the U.S. Navy wins a decisive victory at the Battle of Leyte Gulf. In December, Germany launches its final offensive in western Europe, known as the Battle of the Bulge, but it soon falters.

1945 The German army, attacked by Soviet troops in the east and by American and British soldiers in the west, retreats toward Berlin. On April 30, Adolf Hitler commits suicide. On May 7, Germany surrenders. Allied troops capture Okinawa in May and prepares to invade Japan. In August, after atomic bombs are dropped on Hiroshima and Nagasaki, Japan surrenders, ending World War II.

FURTHER READING

Atkinson, Rick. *The Guns at Last Light: The War in Western Europe, 1944-1945*. New York: Henry Holt, 2013.

Busha, James P. *The Fight in the Clouds: The Extraordinary Combat Experience of P-51 Mustang Pilots during World War II*. Minneapolis, Minn.: Zenith Press, 2014.

Hastings, Max. *Inferno: The World at War, 1939-1945*. New York: Alfred A. Knopf, 2011.

McManus, John C. *The Dead and Those About to Die: D-Day: The Big Red One at Omaha Beach*. New York: NAL Caliber, 2014.

Roberts, Andrew. *The Storm of War: A New History of the Second World War*. New York: HarperCollins, 2011.

Scott, James. *The War Below: The Story of Three Submarines That Battled Japan*. New York: Simon & Schuster, 2013.

Wukovits, John. *One Square Mile of Hell: The Battle for Tarawa*. New York: NAL Caliber, 2006.

INTERNET RESOURCES

http://memory.loc.gov/ammem/collections/maps/wwii/ index.html

The Library of Congress presents a huge collection of World War II military situation maps from 1944 and 1945.

http://www.pbs.org/thewar/

Learn about World War II from people who were there. This PBS site supplements the documentary *The War* by Ken Burns.

http://www.ushmm.org/

The website of United States Holocaust Memorial Museum contains a wealth of stories, facts, and photos.

http://www.theatlantic.com/infocus/pages/ww2/

This site by *The Atlantic* magazine offers 900 of the war's most captivating photos. See images from the front lines and the home front.

http://www.nationalww2museum.org/index.html

The National WWII Museum provides fact sheets, news, and online exhibits for a variety of war-related topics.

INDEX

Numbers in ***bold italics*** refer to captions.

 **SERIES GLOSSARY**

blockade—an effort to cut off supplies, war material, or communications by a particular area, by force or the threat of force.

guerrilla warfare—a type of warfare in which a small group of combatants, such as armed civilians, use hit-and-run tactics to fight a larger and less mobile traditional army. The purpose is to weaken an enemy's strength through small skirmishes, rather than fighting pitched battles where the guerrillas would be at a disadvantage.

intelligence—the analysis of information collected from various sources in order to provide guidance and direction to military commanders.

logistics—the planning and execution of movements by military forces, and the supply of those forces.

salient—a pocket or bulge in a fortified line or battle line that projects into enemy territory.

siege—a military blockade of a city or fortress, with the intent of conquering it at a later stage.

tactics—the science and art of organizing a military force, and the techniques for using military units and their weapons to defeat an enemy in battle.